Bat's Band

Gregory Michaels
Illustrations by Dominic Catalano

HAMPTON-BROWN

A cat with a bag comes in.
He is in the band.

2

An ant with a can comes in.
She is in the band.

A fox with a box comes in.
He is in the band.

A bat with a hat comes in.

She is in the band.

Tap. Tap. Tap.

A cricket with wings comes in.
He sings in the band!